cloverleaf books™

Community Helpers

Let's Meet a Police Officer

Gina Bellisario

illustrated by Cale Atkinson

MILLBROOK PRESS · MINNEAPOLIS

For police officers and their families —G.B.

Millbrook Press
A division of Lerner Publishing Group, Inc.
241 First Avenue North
Minneapolis, MN 55401 U.S.A.

Website address: www.lernerbooks.com

Main body text set in Slappy Inline 18/28.
Typeface provided by T26.

Library of Congress Cataloging-in-Publication Data

Bellisario, Gina.
Let's meet a police officer / by Gina Bellisario ; illustrated by Cale Atkinson.
p. cm. — (Cloverleaf books™ : community helpers)
Includes index.
ISBN: 978-0-7613-9024-4 (lib. bdg. : alk. paper)
1. Police. 2. Occupations. I. Title.
HV7921.B4275 2013
363.2—dc23 2012010393

Manufactured in the United States of America
1 - BP - 12/31/12

TABLE OF CONTENTS

Chapter One

Officer Gabby's Assignment

Today our class is having a visitor. We're going to find out what a **police officer** does. We invited Officer Gabby. She works at our school.

"I keep our neighborhood safe," says Officer Gabby.
"And our school!" says Madeline.

Officer Gabby is a **school resource officer**. That's her assignment. Making students safe is her job.

She stops cars at the **crosswalk**.

And she warns us about **strangers.**

Every police officer has an assignment. Different assignments have different jobs. Traffic officers give tickets. Field training officers teach new officers. School resource officers help students.

"Did you get your assignment from police school?" asks Phoebe.

"From my police department," says Officer Gabby. "First, I was a **patrol officer**. It was part of my training. I worked hard. Then I got a new assignment."

Officers start training in school. Their school is a police academy. They go to this school after they finish high school. They study the law there. They practice directing traffic and other skills. The academy helps them get ready for their assignments.

We're happy she did!

Chapter Two

Officer Ken and a K-9

Most officers wear a **police uniform**. Special clothes and tools are a part of this uniform.

"10-51 at 1422 Pine Street." Officer Gabby's uniform is **talking!**

"What's that noise?" asks Beckett.

"My **police radio**," she says. "Officer Ken is on patrol. The radio is how he shares **information**."

Officers talk over a police radio. They use numbers. Some numbers are paired with 10. The pairs are instructions. "10-51" is "tow truck needed." "10-4" is "I hear you." Using numbers is a fast way of talking.

Officer Ken works in the neighborhood. He drives a **police car**.

Some patrol officers use helicopters or boats. Others ride bicycles or motorcycles. Still others work on horseback!

Police cars have technology tools. A radio sends messages. A camera records what officers see. There's even room for a computer. Officers look up cars' license plate numbers. They also type reports.

Patrol officers get information on the go. They use **technology** to help them do their jobs.

Officer Ken has a **K-9** partner. K-9 partners are also called **police dogs**. Officer Ken's K-9 partner is named **Badge**.

Sniffing out things is a K-9 partner's job. Badge finds people and hidden objects. And he wears a uniform too!

K-9 partners use a special tool. That tool is their nose! A dog's sense of smell is a thousand times stronger than a human's. Police dogs can follow a trail for miles. They can pick up a scent underground. They can even smell things underwater!

Chapter Three

Team Safety

"Do officers have people partners?" asks Ben.

"Many do," says Officer Gabby. "We also work with officers in other towns, cities, states, and countries. By teaming up, we can keep you safer."

Police officers are part of a community. A community is a group of people who live in the same city, town, or neighborhood.

"Go Team Safety!" says Ben.

Not all police officers work in a neighborhood. State police patrol highways. They keep **roads safe** across the state.

FBI agents protect the country. They gather information to fight crime. And they help catch people who break the law.

FBI Headquarters are in Washington, D.C. But FBI agents work around the world. The agents collect fingerprints. They watch areas for crime. They also use science to solve cases.

Even we help **Team Safety!**

We buckle our **seat belts**.

We stand up against **bullying**.

When there's an emergency, we dial **9-1-1**.

Officer Gabby makes our neighborhood **safe**.
So we give our neighborhood helper a hand too!

On Assignment

Officer Gabby's assignment is to be a school resource officer. Teaching safety is her job. Do you want to help people too? Team up with your classmates or family members. Help one another. Go on assignment!

What you need:

a group of classmates or family members
(your group can be big or small—any number of people will do)
a note card for every person in your group
a pencil for every person in your group

What to do:

1) Hand out one note card and one pencil to each person. Have each person choose an assignment for himself or herself. Choose an assignment for yourself too! Someone who loves pets might be a pet care officer. He or she could care for any household or classroom pets. Someone who's very organized might be a cleanup officer. He or she could pick up litter from the classroom floor or put away games and toys.

2) Have everyone write the name of his or her assignment on a note card.

3) Decide exactly what jobs everyone will do. Every assignment should have at least three specific jobs. For example, a pet care officer could walk the dog, fill the dog's food bowl, and make sure the dog's water bowl has fresh water in it. A cleanup officer might pick up five pieces of litter or stray toys that he or she finds on the floor, wipe off the surfaces of all the desks or tables in one room of a school or home, and wipe off the dry-erase board or wash dishes at the end of the day.

4) Have everyone list his or her jobs underneath his or her assignment name.

5) Finally, set aside one day for everyone to complete his or her jobs. Congratulate fellow officers once everyone's jobs are done. Way to go, team!

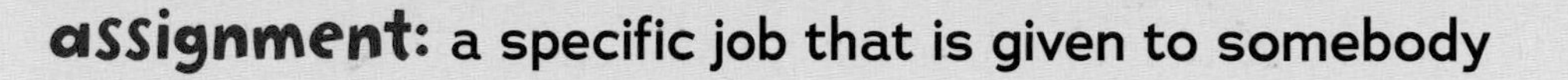

GLOSSARY

assignment: a specific job that is given to somebody

community: a group of people who live in the same area

crime: something that is against the law

crosswalk: a place where people can safely walk across a street

emergency: a problem that needs attention fast

law: a rule made by the government

9-1-1: a phone number to call during emergencies

patrol: to move around an area to protect it or to keep watch on people

technology: tools made by people to improve life, such as computers and cell phones

uniform: a special set of clothes worn by all the members of a particular group. Police officers, nurses, soldiers, and letter carriers wear uniforms.

TO LEARN MORE

BOOKS

Anderson, Sheila. *Police Station.* Minneapolis: Lerner Publications Company, 2008.
Check out this fun and simple introduction to police stations.

Askew, Amanda. *Police Officer.* Irvine, CA: QEB Publishing, 2010.
Meet a police officer named Anita and read about the problems she solves in her neighborhood.

Hoffman, Mary Ann. *Police Dogs.* New York: Gareth Stevens Publishing, 2011.
Find out how dogs help police officers stop crime.

WEBSITES

Barrett Township Police Department
http://www.barrett.monroe.pa.us/Police/kids.htm
Visit this site to find pictures to color, Internet safety tips, and a fun quiz about police officers.

The Federal Bureau of Investigation
http://www.fbi.gov/fun-games/kids/kids
Learn about the FBI, get important safety information, and play FBI-themed games.

McGruff
http://mcgruff.com
This website is from the National Crime Prevention Council. It has safety tips from McGruff, the crime dog. It also has lots of games and advice about things such as bullying and playing outside.

LERNER eSOURCE™
Expand learning beyond the printed book. Download free, complementary educational resources for this book from our website, www.lerneresource.com.

INDEX